Breaking Traditions

Dr. Jake Williams Jr

Cover art and Editing by:
La' Won D. Williams
Tanzanieka Harris
Barbara W. Williams

Unless otherwise indicated, all Scripture quotations are taken from the King James Version of the Bible.

ISBN: 978-0-9986590-0-8
First printing: March 2017

FOR MORE BOOKS OR INFORMATION CONTACT:
Dr. Jake Williams Jr, Pastor
Jesus World Outreach Center, Inc.
PO Box 41424
Fayetteville, NC 28309
(910) 823-4849

Please visit our website at:
www.jwoc.org

DEDICATION

I want to dedicate this book to my church members that have remained faithful to the vision. Who have believed in my wife and me to be God sent, and have allowed us to pastor them by feeding them with knowledge and understanding. Thank you for the love and support.

CONTENTS

ACKNOWLEDGMENTS

God the Father, His Son Jesus and the Holy Spirit for guiding me and reminding me to always be steadfast and unmovable.

My wife, Barbara and our children for their love, support and patience.

My parents, Jake and Ruthie Mae Williams, for giving me life and love, by training me in the way that I should go.

My pastors, Elisha and Phyllis Lawson, for believing in me and encouraging me by saying, there are books in you, write.

INTRODUCTION

Mark 7:9, 13 says, *"And he [Jesus] said unto them, Full well ye reject the commandment of God, that ye may keep your own tradition. 13 Making the word of God of none effect through your tradition, which ye have delivered: and many such like things do ye"*.

Jesus was letting the Pharisees, certain of the scribes and the people know that not all traditions are good, especially when they cause you to not keep the commandments of God.

This book is written to anyone that has an ear to hear, and it's about breaking certain religious traditions by taking another look, with a different view. This different view is only for your consideration, but change, it begins with you. Let's look at some traditions that you may have thought to be true.

These traditions that I will be talking about can nullify or make your faith weak causing you to not receive the full promises of God. Perhaps some of you have heard of these traditions all of your lives, either in church, or through other people even family members, but have never taken the time yourselves to research the scriptures to see whether these things are biblically true. Acts 17:11 says, *"…searched the scriptures daily, whether those things were so [true]"*. I'm asking that you read this book with an open mind, and a different view of these traditions that I will be talking about. Jesus said, *"For unto whomsoever much is given, of him shall be much required" (Luke 12:48)*. I believe what I have written in this book I have been led, guided, and inspired by the Holy Spirit to write it and to share. Romans 12:2 says *"And be not conformed to this world: but be ye transformed by the renewing of your mind, that ye may prove what is that good, and acceptable, and perfect, will of God"*. We Christians must learn to change our way of thinking, and we do that by renewing our minds with truth. Well what is truth? Jesus said in John 17:17 *"...thy word is truth"*. So we see the word of God is truth, and that's what we renew our minds with. Proverbs 9:9 says, *"Give instruction to a wise man, and he will be yet wiser: teach a just man, and he will increase in learning"*. Daniel 12:4 says, *"...O Daniel, shut up the words, and seal the book, even to the time of the end: many shall run to and fro, and knowledge shall be increased"*. I believe that there comes a time when we all must be brought to the truth, and then we are given the choice to accept the truth or to reject it. As time goes forward God said knowledge shall increase. Do you have an ear to hear? If what I have written in this book helps you with spiritual insight, receive it; if it doesn't, trash it, and that's all I have to say about that. Proverbs 18:13 says, *He that answereth a matter before he heareth it, it is folly [foolish] and shame unto him.* Don't be foolish! Hear the whole matter by reading the entire book before judging the subjects in the table of contents. Remember change, it begins with you. With these things in mind let's get started.

DEFINITIONS

Socrates, a Greek philosopher said *"in order for two people to discuss any topic adequately, they must first define their terms, so that both will know what the other is talking about"*.

Words have a way of meaning different things to different people. First, if you are going to understand what I am talking about in this book, you must first understand the definition of certain words, and how I will be using them.

The definition of words that I will be using in this book, to help you better understand:

Old and New Testaments - are really Old and New Covenants. The word, testament, is <u>Latin</u> *for the word Covenant.* (from the Strong's Concordance).

The Hebrew word for covenant is Berith which means to *"<u>bind</u>"* or *"<u>to bond</u>". (from the Strong's Concordance).*

The Greek word for covenant is Diatheke which means *"<u>will</u>"* or *"<u>testament</u>"*, which are legal terms. *(from the Strong's Concordance).*

Covenant – *"1. an agreement between two or more parties to do or not do something specified.2. undertaking, commitment, guarantee, warrant, pledge, promise, bond".* (from dictionary.com).

Dispensation – *"a certain order, system, or arrangement; a special period of time that has a beginning and an end before the next time period begins".* (from dictionary.com, and the Strong's Concordance).

Example of a Dispensation: <u>*2016*</u> *was a dispensation, it had a start date of January 1, and an end date of December 31 before the next time period* <u>*2017*</u> *begins.*

Kingdom of God – *"righteousness, peace and joy; God's way of doing things"*. (Romans 14:17) (KJV).

SEVEN DISPENSATIONS

Second, if you are going to understand what I'm talking about in this book, you must understand the dispensations of the bible. By understanding this, I believe it will help you to understand where I am coming from in this book.

The Bible is divided into seven dispensations: *(remember the definition?)*

1 <u>Innocence</u> – *from God's creation of man* <u>Gen 1:26, 27</u>, <u>Gen 2:7, 25</u> / *to judgment, man expelled from the garden of Eden* <u>Gen 3:17-19</u>, <u>Gen 3:22-24</u>.

2 <u>Conscience</u> – *from Cain murders Abel* <u>Gen 4:2-15</u> / *to the flood* <u>Gen 7:11-12, 23</u>

3 <u>Government</u> – *from Noah worships God, and receives a covenant* <u>Gen 8:20-22</u> / *to the tower of Babel, Confusion of man's language* <u>Gen 11:5-9</u>.

4 <u>Promise</u> – *from God calls Abram and gives him promises* <u>Gen 12:1-7</u>; <u>13:14-17</u>; <u>15:5</u>*and those promises repeated to Isaac & Jacob* <u>Gen 26:1-5</u>; <u>28:10-15</u> / *to Bondage in Egypt* <u>Ex 1:7-14</u>; <u>2:23-25</u>.

5 <u>The Law</u> – *from The Law is given to Moses* <u>Ex 19:1-8</u> to Jesus, the death of the Cross <u>John 19:30</u>.

6 <u>Grace</u> – *from Christ ascends and sends the Holy Spirit Acts 1:1-9; Acts 2:1-4 / to we shall meet the Lord in the air 1 Thes4:16-17.*

7 <u>Kingdom or The Reign of Christ</u> – *from Jesus Christ returns to earth as King of kings Matt 25:31-34 / to Judgment of Satan and the rebellion cast into the lake of fire. Rev 20:10-15.*

CHAPTER 1

Matthew, Mark, Luke and John: Old Testament <u>NOT</u> New Testament:

Matthew, Mark, Luke and John have been traditionally called the first four books of the New Testament, traditionally. But technically Matthew, Mark, Luke and John are the last four books of the Old Testament. The book of Acts should be the first book of the New Testament, and the book of John should be the last book of the Old Testament. I believe if it was put together this way, when people read it, it would be much more understandable. Follow me as I explain with a different view, and you will see it clearly.

When Jesus walked the earth and ministered, He did so during the time of the dispensation of the law. Most people think when they're reading Matthew, Mark, Luke and John, they are reading New Testament, but technically they are not, they are actually reading Old Testament. God said through the apostle Paul in Galatians 4:4-5 *"But when the fulness of the time was come, God sent forth his Son, made of a woman, made under the law* (meaning during the time of the law), *5 To redeem them that were under the law, that we might receive the adoption of sons".* Matthew, Mark, Luke and John are each an account of Jesus' 33 and one half years of life and ministry while here on the earth, during the time of the law, but redemption for mankind had not been accomplished yet. Some have thought that when Jesus hung on the cross and said, *"...it is finished..." (John 19:30)* He was talking about salvation and man's redemption, but He wasn't. He was only talking about the old covenant dispensation *(the Old Testament),* the law, being finished. Jesus fulfilled it!!! Sure Romans 6:23 says, *"For the wages of sin is death...",* well He could not have been talking about salvation when he said "it is finished" because salvation is based on you believing and confessing that Jesus died for the price of sin, but He not only died, He also rose from the dead, three days later, alive. So, until He went back to heaven, and presented His blood to the Father for the forgiveness of man's sin, mankind was still under the law. God also said through the apostle Paul, *"that no man is justified* (made righteous) *by the law in the sight of God..."* *(Galatians 3:11),* and under the law, no man could be made righteous. There was fault found in the Old Testament with them *(the children of Israel).* Hebrews 8:7-8 says, *"For if that first covenant had been faultless, then should no place have been sought for the second. 8 For finding fault with them, he saith, Behold, the days come, saith the Lord, when I will make a new covenant with the house of Israel...".*

Let's look at the word testament. I believe if you understand this word it will help simplify or make things much clearer for you. The word testament is a legal term, it is Latin for the word covenant which means *"will or testament".* Have you ever heard someone say, or use the phrase, the last *will* and *testament* of John Doe *(just to use a name)*? A will *(a legal document)* is enforced after the death of the testator *(the maker of the will)* not while he or she is still alive. A will is read after the death of the person that made the will *(testator),* not before. There is no way a will can be enforced while the person that made it is still alive. Hebrews 9:15-17 says, "...*he [Jesus] is the mediator of the new testament, that by means of death, for the redemption of the transgressions that were under the first testament* [old testament/covenant] ... *16 For where a testament is, there must also of necessity be the death of the testator. 17 For a testament is of force after men are dead: otherwise it is of no strength at all while the testator liveth*".

A will is a legal document that provides specific instructions as to what is to be done with a person's possessions after their death. Jesus left us *a better covenant* [testament/will], *which was established upon better promises (Hebrews 8:6)*. In this covenant *(will)* He "*has given us all things that pertain to life and godliness...*" *(2 Peter 1:3)*, and that's the New Testament, the dispensation of Grace that did not come until the book of Acts.

Jesus was still alive during Matthew, Mark, Luke and John until the death of the cross. So, that means Matthew, Mark, Luke and John are Old Testament, the law. So, in order to fulfill the law Jesus had to be here during the time of the law. When most people hear the phrase "the law", they automatically think of the "Ten Commandments". The Ten Commandments are only a small part of the law. The dispensation of the law began when Moses received the Ten Commandments and ended with the ascension of Jesus. I will explain more about the Ten Commandments in chapter three.

"*Jesus said I did not come to destroy the law, or the prophets, but to fulfill*" *(Matthew 5:17)*. To fulfill the law, He had to be here during the time of the law. When people read Matthew, Mark, Luke and John they think that they are reading New Testament but again technically they are not. When you read Matthew, Mark, Luke and John, start seeing it as the last four books of the Old Testament, and see the book of Acts as the first book of the New Testament, and I believe it will be much more understandable.

CHAPTER 2

The Lord's Prayer – "Another View" Breaking Tradition:

Have you ever been watching a war or spy movie on television or at the movies and see a guy get shot? While he's dying, he starts quoting the Lord's Prayer, believing that by doing this God will forgive him of all his wrongness. This is very misleading and is far from the truth. That only happens in Hollywood. The Lord's Prayer has never, and will never save or forgive anyone of their wrongness. Let me show you what I'm talking about.

Now that you understand that Matthew, Mark, Luke and John are Old Testament, and the book of Acts is the first book of the New Testament, let's now take another look at what is called the Lord's Prayer from a different view.

Matt. 6:9-13 says, *"After this manner therefore pray ye: Our Father which art in heaven, Hallowed be thy name. 10 Thy kingdom come. Thy will be done in earth, as it is in heaven. 11 Give us this day our daily bread. 12 And forgive us our debts, as we forgive our debtors. 13 And lead us not into temptation, but deliver us from evil:*

For thine is the kingdom, and the power, and the glory, forever Amen".

Traditionally this passage has been called the Lord's Prayer. Some people pray it religiously, and have based their salvation on it all because Jesus prayed it.

I personally don't have any problem with you praying this prayer. But why do something out of tradition? Why continue to do something just because it has always been done that way? If there aren't any spiritual benefits in it, why do it? When you do something out of tradition and not out of biblical truth, it can cause your faith to be weak.

I submit unto you that Jesus did not pray this prayer, so how can it be called "the Lord's Prayer"? If He prayed it then maybe it could be called the Lord's Prayer, but He didn't pray it. He told his disciples to pray it. *"...And He said to them (the disciples), when you pray, say..." (Luke 11:2).*

Why did Jesus tell the disciples to pray this way? He told them *(the disciples)* to pray this way, as a simplified way to finish out the last days of the Old Covenant dispensation *(the law)*. *Luke 11:2* states *"...And He said to them (the disciples), when you pray, say..."*. We see here that He didn't pray this way, He told the disciples to pray this way. Some have thought Jesus was telling the whole world to pray this way, when He said *"when you pray, say"*, but He wasn't. He was only talking to the disciples. We can see this in Luke 11:1 which says, *"... as he was praying in a certain place, when he ceased, one of his disciples said unto him, Lord, teach us to pray, as John also taught his disciples. And He said unto them (the disciples), When ye pray, say..."*. Jesus was NOT telling the whole world to pray this way, only the disciples!!!

Don't do things out of tradition because everyone else is doing it that way. Again, doing this can nullify or make your faith weak and prevent you from walking in the fulfilled promises of God. If this prayer was so important for us to pray, why haven't we found anywhere else in the four Gospels or in the New Testament where someone else ever prayed this prayer? The reason why is because it is not a New Testament prayer. It was not meant for the Kingdom age *(The New Covenant dispensation)*. Under the Old Covenant dispensation Jesus told the disciples to pray that the Kingdom of God come, and that they be delivered from evil or literally the evil one *(Satan)*. The Kingdom of God had NOT COME YET during that time *(the law)*. The price for sin had not been paid yet. They had not been delivered from the evil one yet, so they had to pray this way: God send the Kingdom; God deliver us; God let Your will be done on earth as it is in heaven. It was the only way they could pray during the time period they were living in.

When we become born again, we become partakers of the inheritance of the saints in light and at that time we are delivered from the power of darkness (the evil one) and we are translated into the Kingdom of His dear Son. *(Colossians 1:12-13)*. Not trying to be translated someday, in the sweet bye and bye, we are translated now because we have received Jesus as personal Lord and Savior!!! We are now in the Kingdom of God, and we now have Jesus' permission to use His name to take care of Kingdom business, but we must do it God's way. Jesus said, *"...behold the Kingdom of God is within you." (Luke 17:21)*.

The Kingdom of God is *"...righteousness, peace, and joy..." (Romans 14:17)*, It is everything God is, everything God can do, everything God has, and everything God will do. It is God's way of doing things. We must change our way of thinking and do things God's way, because *"as He is, so are we in this world" (1 John 4:17)*. If we want to receive Kingdom benefits, then we *(the Christians)* must pray according to the New Covenant dispensation, and NOT pray what is called "The Lord's Prayer" out of tradition.

Now that you have this understanding, let's look at *"how to pray"* under the New Covenant dispensation. Jesus did not leave the disciples ignorant, when He moved them from the Old to the New Covenant dispensation, He taught them how to pray. This is how Jesus told the disciples and us to pray under the New Covenant dispensation: we pray to the Father in the name of Jesus.

John 16:16-24 says, *"A little while, and ye shall not see me: and again, a little while, and ye shall see me, because I go to the Father. 17 Then said some of his disciples among themselves, What is this that he saith unto us, A little while, and ye shall not see me: and again, a little while, and ye shall see me: and, Because I go to the Father? 18 They said therefore, What is this that he saith, A little while? we cannot tell what he saith. 19 Now Jesus knew that they were desirous to ask him, and said unto them, Do ye enquire among yourselves of that I said, A little while, and ye shall not see me: and again, a little while, and ye shall see me? 20 Verily, verily, I say unto you, That ye shall weep and lament, but the world shall rejoice: and ye shall be sorrowful, but your sorrow shall be turned into joy. 21 A woman when she is in travail hath sorrow, because her hour is come: but as soon as she is delivered of the child, she remembereth no more the anguish, for joy that a man is born into the world. 22 And ye now therefore have sorrow: but I will see you again, and your heart shall rejoice, and your joy no man taketh from you. 23 And in that day ye shall ask me nothing. Verily, verily, I say unto you, Whatsoever ye shall ask the Father in my name, he will give it you. 24 Hitherto have ye asked nothing in my name: ask, and ye shall receive, that your joy may be full".*

Up until this time the disciples had never asked God for anything. They didn't have to, they just asked Jesus. When they needed something to eat, they asked Jesus. When they needed money to pay the taxes, they asked Jesus.When they were on the boat and a storm of wind came up, you didn't hear the disciples praying to God.

They woke up Jesus and said *"Master, carest thou not that we perish? And He arose, and rebuked the wind"* (Mark 4:38). They had God, Emmanuel, which means *"God with us"*, with them the whole time". Let's go back to John the 16th chapter and take a closer look at what Jesus was saying. Look at verse *22 "And ye now therefore have sorrow..."* look at the word *now*, the word *now* indicates a period of time, which is present tense, present time, which they were living in, the time period of the law. Jesus was letting them know, right now you have sorrow because I'm going to die, but it's ok you'll see me again. He was talking about His resurrection, *"you'll see Me again"* when I'm raised from the dead.

Now look at verse 23, *"And in that day ye shall ask me nothing"*. What day was he talking about? Look at the words *"and in that day"* they indicate future tense. When in the future? After I'm raised from the dead, after I ascend back to heaven, after I sit down at the right hand of the Father and begin My intersession on your behalf, *"and in that day"* you shall ask Me nothing. That's the day He was talking about, the future. Jesus goes on to say, *"Whatsoever ye shall ask the Father in my name, he will give it you"*. You don't pray and ask Jesus to do anything for you, but it's ok to talk to Him, and thank Him for the work He did for you on cavalry. There is nothing wrong with doing that, but when you desire something, He goes on to say, *"whatsoever"* you *"ask the Father"* in *"My name"* *"He"* *(the Father)* will give it to you. Well, what is the flip side of that statement, *if you don't ask the Father in My name* it won't be given to you. Notice what Jesus goes on to say in verse 24: *"Hitherto have ye asked nothing in my name:"* *"Hitherto"* means up to now, so He was saying to the disciples, up to now you never had to ask for anything in My name. The reason why is because the Father had not yet given Him *(Jesus)* a name that is above every name. He *(Jesus)* hadn't earned the name above every name yet, because He had not defeated satan, death, hell, and the grave. Jesus goes on to say to them, but after I go back to heaven and sit down at the right hand of the Father, ask the Father in My name and He will give it to you, because I have now earned the name that is above every name, and I'm giving you permission to use My name to take care of Kingdom business. Praise God!!!

We have Jesus' permission to use His name to take care of any kind of Kingdom business, but we must do it the way He has instructed. Under the New Covenant dispensation, prayer is based on the known word of God. In order to pray an effective prayer you must know what God has promised you and then you must believe it and say it.

Jesus told us to *"...have faith in God" (Mark 11:22)*. Then He went on to say in *Mark 11:23-24 "For verily I say unto you, That whosoever shall say unto this mountain, Be thou removed, and be thou cast into the sea; and shall not doubt in his heart, but shall believe that those things which he saith shall come to pass; he shall have whatsoever he saith. 24 Therefore I say unto you, What things soever ye desire, when ye pray, believe that ye receive them, and ye shall have them"*.

Notice Jesus used the words say, believe and saith in these two verses. He is trying to get the disciples to understand that the words they speak are life, and they will have whatsoever they say, if they believe it. That's why He said, have faith in God. We are dealt the measure of faith when we become born again *(Romans 12:3)*. We have the God kind of faith, we have the same faith that God used to speak the world into creation. We can't speak anything else into creation, but we can speak what we want to happen in our lives. So, He was telling His disciples, believe it when you speak it and it will come to pass.

Let's go back to verse *24 "Therefore I say unto you, What things soever ye desire, when ye pray, believe that ye receive them, and ye shall have them".* Question, what did Jesus say you will have in this verse? He said the only thing that you will have are the things that you believed that you received when you prayed. Not after you have prayed, but right now while you are praying *(present tense)* you must believe that you receive whatever it is you are asking for. Now your asking must be in line with *"things that pertain to life and godliness" (2 Peter 1:3).* This is how prayer works in the Kingdom of God under the New Covenant dispensation, and that's how we are instructed to pray. Prayer is not just saying a bunch of words that sound good, but it's saying or agreeing with the same things that God has already said or promised. The passage known as the Lord's Prayer will not work for you *(Christians)* in the New Covenant dispensation, so why pray it, even out of tradition? When you pray this prayer, you are sowing the wrong things into your spirit, because faith cometh by hearing even when you are hearing it from yourself.

CHAPTER 3

The Ten Commandments - Not for a Christian today
under the New Covenant:

When the children of Israel left Egypt, they had no laws to
govern them, until God gave the Ten Commandments to
Moses. These Ten Commandments were only a small part
of *the law*, and they were given to spiritually dead men. The
children of Israel were not born again, because Jesus did
not come until hundreds of years later to pay the price for
sin. They were to live by these Ten Commandments, and
as time went on more Commandments were added. The
dispensation of *the law* is considered from the giving of the
Ten Commandments to Moses, to the ascension of Jesus.
Most people think that God gave the children of Israel
only ten laws to keep. Not so!!! He couldn't give them too
much at one time, they would fail. Just as if you were given
too much to do or keep at one time, you would fail. The
children of Israel were no different, yet they were God's
chosen people. These people were bound by the letter of
the law, there was no grace. *If a man was caught stealing, his
wife and kids were stoned to death along with him (Joshua 7:19-26);
if a person was caught in adultery, all involved, innocent or not were*

put to death, Deuteronomy 22:22; a person with leprosy could no longer live in the camp, that person had to live alone outside the camp (Leviticus 13:45). If a wife jumped into a fight that her husband was having with a man, and she grabbed the man by his secrets (private parts) *her hand would be cut off (Deuteronomy 25:11-12).* There wasn't any grace, it was the law. What if we were still under these penalties today? There would be less people in the world today, don't you think?

Thank God that we Christians are not living under the dispensation of the law, but we live under the dispensation of Grace. Grace is God's unmerited favor, meaning we don't deserve His goodness, mercy or forgiveness, but He gave it anyway. Christians are not bound by the Ten Commandments, that's under the law. God said through the apostle Paul in *Galatians 3:11-12 "But that no man is justified* (made righteous) *by the law in the sight of God, it is evident: for, The just shall live by faith. And the law is not of faith: but, The man that doeth them shall live in them".* We *(Christians)* are the just *(declared righteous)*, and Christians under the New Testament are commanded to live by faith, faith in God, not by the law, because the law is not of faith. That means we must believe that God will do what He said He'll do. God is faithful, and He requires us to live by faith. He said in *Hebrews 11:6 "for without faith it is impossible to please him...".* So, by faith we must take Him at His word. We *(Christians)* don't live by the Ten Commandments. We have been given a new commandment and we are called to live by it. It is called, *"the law of love".* Jesus said, *"A new commandment I give unto you, That ye love one another; as I have loved you, that ye also love one another" (John 13:34).* We *(Christians)* are commanded to keep this law, and this law only. What law? The law of love, not the Ten Commandments. Under the New Testament, the Ten Commandments are not for a Christian today. Am I saying it's ok to steal, kill, commit adultery, murder, bear false witness, and so on? No!!! What I am saying is that if you live by the law of love then you won't steal, kill, commit adultery, murder, bear false witness, and so on. You won't do these things, because love will always compel you to do what is right. Romans 13:8-10 says, *"Owe no man anything, but to love one another: for he that "loveth" another hath fulfilled the law. For this, Thou shalt not commit adultery, Thou shalt not kill, Thou shalt not steal, Thou shalt not bear false witness, Thou shalt not covet; and if there be any other commandment, it is briefly comprehended in this saying, namely, Thou shalt love thy neighbour as thyself. Love worketh no ill to his neighbour: therefore "love" is the fulfilling of the law".* Jesus said, *"If a man love me, he will keep my words" (John 14:23).* Love is your motivator, and it will cause you to keep all of God's Commandments and not just ten. *"…if God so loved us, we ought also to love one another…, …God is love…, …as he is, so are we in this world" (1 John 4:11,16-17).* If God is love, that means we are love also, because as He is so are we, and in this world, we are love, and we must live by the law of love and not by the Ten Commandments. The law of love supersedes *(to make obsolete)* the Ten Commandments, that's why I say that the Ten Commandments are not for a Christian today under the New Covenant.

CHAPTER 4

Jesus and the Disciples were Poor – Now That's a Lie!!!

Perhaps some of you have heard people say that Jesus and the disciples were poor people and they didn't have any earthly wealth or goods, so why should we. That's not biblically true. I've even heard people say, because Jesus didn't have any material goods, I don't want any material goods. People that believe this way have gotten some wrong teaching somewhere in their lives, and now because their believing is wrong they will never own any material goods. So, they will rent all their lives never owning a home, never owning an automobile subjecting their family to public transportation, waiting for a ride in the cold during the winter and in the heat during the summer. That's about the dumbest thing I've ever heard. I'm going to show you in the scriptures that Jesus was rich, He was not a poor man, and his disciples were not poor people, He was surrounded by disciples that already had plenty in life.

2 Corinthians 8:9 says, "*For ye know the grace of our Lord Jesus Christ, that, though he was rich, yet for your sakes he became*

15

poor, that ye through his poverty might be rich". Notice what the scripture says; *"though he was rich, yet for your sakes he became poor"*. In heaven, before Jesus left, we can see that the city and the streets were made of pure gold, and the book of Revelation gives us a small glimpse of what heaven looks like. Most people say that the streets in heaven are paved with gold, which means that there is gold overlaid on top of something else underneath. Not so!!! I submit unto you the bible says that the streets were made of pure gold, not an overlay of gold. Revelation 21:18 says, *"… the city was pure gold, like unto clear glass…"*, and Revelation 21:21 says, *"…the street of the city was pure gold, as it were transparent glass"*. So, we see here when Jesus left heaven He came from wealth, He was rich, and He was more than just rich in mercy as some preachers preach. Now when it says *"he became poor"*, this is not poor the way we think of poor. Imagine two people, one has $100 billion dollars and the other only has $2 million dollars, now you would consider the person with $2 million dollars to be poor compared to the person with $100 billion dollars. But $2 million dollars is not poor. That's how we must see Jesus, what He had in heaven *(example $100 billion dollars)* compared to what He had here on earth *(example $2 million dollars)* you would consider Him poor here on earth, compared to what he had in heaven, but he wasn't poor the way we view poor. Question!!! What do you think Joseph and Mary did with all the wealth that the wise men brought to Jesus shortly after his birth? *"And when they* [the wise men] *were come into the house, they saw the young child with Mary his mother, and fell down, and worshipped him: and when they had opened their treasures, they presented unto him gifts; gold, and frankincense, and myrrh" (Matthew 2:11)*. Now what do you think happened to all that earthly wealth? Do you think Joseph and Mary just went on a spending spree? Do you think Joseph and Mary just misused all that wealth the wise men gave to them? Not so!!! You can see here from this passage of scripture that Jesus was born into earthly wealth, he did not grow up a poor man. Now compared to what He had in heaven, cities and streets made of pure gold and you now consider what the wise men gave Him, you would call Him poor here on earth. Because we don't have any cities or streets made of pure gold here on this earth.

Remember I told you that Jesus was surrounded by disciples that already had plenty in life, and they were not poor people. Follow me and let's see what the scriptures say; Mark 1:16-20 says, *"Now as he [Jesus] walked by the sea of Galilee, he saw Simon and Andrew his brother casting a net into the sea: for they were fishers".*

Now let me stop here and explain because the Bible used the term here, *they were "fishers".* It didn't say they were fishing, It said they were "fishers". The term *"fishers"* identifies their profession, how they made their living, the business that they owned. This is not a play on words!!! This is very important that you understand what it was saying. They owned a fishing business, it was their business. Who's business? Simon and his brother Andrew, they had a family owned fishing business. The scripture was highlighting what they had, not what they were doing, *they were "fishers".* It shows these guys had something in life, they were not poor, they owned a fishing business.

Let's read on, the next verse says, *17 "And Jesus said unto them, Come ye after me, and I will make you to become fishers of men".* Jesus was saying to them, follow me, and if you stick with me I'm going give you a new profession, *"fishers of men". 18 "And straightway they forsook their nets, and followed him. 19 And when he had gone a little further thence, he saw James the son of Zebedee, and John his brother, who also were in the ship mending their nets. 20 And straightway he called them: and they left their father Zebedee in the ship with the hired servants, and went after him".* Here's another family fishing business, James, his brother John, their father and *"the hired servants".* Do you see it? Poor folks don't have servants working for them, in fact the poor are usually the ones serving the rich. Here are two more disciples that decided to follow Jesus and they were not poor. They had other people working for them. If you have other people working for you then I would think you have to have money to pay them.

Luke 5:10 says, *"And so was also James, and John, the sons of Zebedee, which were partners with Simon. And Jesus said unto Simon, Fear not; from henceforth thou shalt catch men".* Check that out, the fishing business was so good and prosperous, Simon and his brother Andrew, and James and his brother John they teamed up and were in partnership together. If you are in business and going to be in partnership with someone else, you both must bring money to the table, so you see once again these men were not poor.

Matthew 9:9 says, *"...Jesus saw a man, named Matthew, sitting at the receipt of custom: and he saith unto him, Follow me. And he arose, and followed him".* Matthew 10:3 says, *"...Matthew the publican* [tax collector]..." . Here Jesus called Matthew the tax collector to be one of his disciples, why? Because he had something. You and I know all tax collectors have money, there are no poor tax collectors. Here's another man that had something.

One of Jesus disciples, Luke by name, was a physician, a doctor. Colossians 4:14 says, *"Luke, the beloved physician, and Demas, greet you".* I'm sure he wasn't poor, the man was a doctor.

And there is Judas Iscarlot, the disciple that betrayed Jesus, the man was a thief. He was only in it for his own benefit, what he could get out of it. John 12:6 says, *"...he* [Judas] *was a thief, and had the bag, and bare what was put therein".* Jesus and the disciples had so much financially, that they had to have a treasurer in the group to carry the bag. Judas had the task of keeping the bag, and the contents of the bag, but the man was a thief. He was stealing out of the bag and none of the other disciples knew it. Only Jesus knew it and He knew it by the Spirit. Now there has to be a whole lot in the bag in order for someone to be stealing out of it and no one notices any money missing. If you only have two things in the bag and one of them is missing, everyone is going to know that something is missing. Jesus and the disciples had plenty, they were not lacking.

Again Jesus and His disciples were not poor people. Jesus was led by the Spirit to choose people that already had something established in life. People who could afford to leave their families and yet their families would still be provided for. Remember when Jesus was talking to the young rich ruler in the 10th chapter of Mark, and Jesus told him to do something, and the young man couldn't do it. Jesus said to the young man, verse *21 "...sell whatsoever thou hast, and give to the poor, and thou shalt have treasure in heaven: and come, take up the cross, and follow me. 22 And he was sad at that saying, and went away grieved: for he had great possessions". (Mark 10:21-22)*. I can imagine the disciples standing there with a dumbfounded look on their faces when they heard the next thing Jesus said in verses 23 and 24 *"And Jesus looked round about, and saith unto his disciples, How hardly shall they that have riches enter into the kingdom of God! 24 And the disciples were astonished at his words" (Mark 10:23-24)*. Why were the disciples *"astonished at His words"?* I'll tell you why, because they also had riches. He goes on to say to them in verses 25 and 26 *"It is easier for a camel to go through the eye of a needle, than for a rich man to enter into the kingdom of God. 26 And they were astonished out of measure, saying among themselves, who then can be saved?" (Mark 10:25-26)*. Now I wasn't there, but I'm sure the disciples looked at Jesus like He was crazy when He said that to them, because they also were rich men. Notice the scripture didn't say this time they were just astonished, but *"they were astonished out of measure"* at what He said. They went on to say, if the rich can't get in *"who then can be saved?"* The reason they asked this question, and had such a dumbfounded look on their faces, is because they were rich men, and they wanted to know if they were going to get in.

Jesus knew that these men could afford to leave their homes, and their businesses will still prosper and provide for themselves and their families for the next three and a half years. The disciples had something going for themselves and Jesus knew it. Jesus didn't just go down by the seashore and get a bunch of drunks and say come on guys follow me and I'm going to make you fishers of men. No, No, No!!! He surrounded himself with people that already had something established in life.

It wouldn't be fair for Jesus to require those men to come follow Him for three and half years, and their families would not be able to provide for themselves. These men already had something established in life that would sustain their families.

For three and a half years Jesus took on caring for thirteen grown adults to include Himself. During this time, He clothed them, housed them, and fed them. Poor folks can't do that!!! In three and a half years you know they wore out clothes, and sandals walking in the desert from place to place. Yet He provided for them, because it wouldn't be fair for them to provide for themselves when He said to them, come follow me. How many of you would be able to take on thirteen grown adults to include yourself, clothing them, housing them, and feeding them for three and a half years? Again, poor folks can't do that!!!

CHAPTER 5

Women Keep Silence in the Church – Why!!!

1 Corinthians 14:34 "Let your women keep silence in the churches: for it is not permitted unto them to speak; but they are commanded to be under obedience, as also saith the law".

If you took this passage of scripture at face value you would think that all women must keep silent in the churches. Preachers have taken this passage of scripture and have preached it for years, saying that women are not supposed to preach nor teach, they are to keep silent in the church. Many books have been written on this topic, but the sad thing is that even today so many preachers are still preaching this nonsense. This is not what Paul was saying in this particular scripture at all. Sometimes you have to read the scripture above the scripture that you're reading and read the scripture below it. You may even have to read two or three chapters to get clarity. Also, sometimes you might have to look up the meaning of words, even the Greek word to know what the writer is saying. I'm going to show you in the scripture exactly what Paul was talking about when he made the statement *"let your women keep silence in the churches"*. If you would read from verse 33 to verse 35, the scripture explains itself, why Paul said this, and it identifies who he is talking about when he said it. He wasn't saying women as in all females, he was saying women as in wives, you can see this in the scripture;

1 Corinthians 14:34-35 says, *"Let your women keep silence in the churches: for it is not permitted unto them to speak; but they are commanded to be under obedience as also saith the law. 35 And if they will learn any thing, let them ask their husbands at home: for it is a shame for women to speak in the church".*

Now let's dissect these two passages of scripture here, because this is crazy to think that a woman is supposed to keep silence in the church today under the *law of love (John 13:34)*. Let's look at the Greek word for woman. The Greek word for woman is *gunē* or *goo-nay'* and this word means *women* and *wife*. It is the same Greek word for both *women* and *wife*, it doesn't tell you in the translation what kind of woman, a married woman or single woman. So which one is the writer talking about when he said *"let your women keep silence in the churches"*? Is he speaking of *women* as in all females, or is he speaking of all married women as in *wives*? The only way to know which one the writer is talking about, is to the read the content of the next verse and it will tell you exactly who he's referring to. 1 Corinthians 14:35 says, *"And if they will learn any thing, let them ask their husbands at home: for it is a shame for women to speak in the church".* It says and *if they will learn anything,* they who *women* or *wives*? Let's read on; let *"them ask their husbands"* at home. Clearly this is talking about a married woman, a wife, because it says *"let them ask their husbands at home".* That is talking about a husband and wife, so when Paul said, *"Let your women keep silence in the churches,"* he was talking about *wives* keep silent, not all woman. Question!!! If he was talking about all women, what is the single woman to do,

22

stay ignorant and not learn because she doesn't have a husband at home to ask?

During that time, there were certain Jewish religious traditions that governed the church. The women sat on one side of the church, and the men sat on the other side; men and women did not sit together. Unfortunately, you can go into some churches today and that tradition is still in practice. Imagine this, the women *(wives)* are sitting on one side of the room, and the men *(husbands)* are sitting on the other side. Paul is up speaking and when a wife didn't understand something that Paul said, she would ask her husband, who was on the other side of the room, for clarification. Now imagine multiple wives continuously asking their husbands for clarification while Paul was up teaching. As a pastor, I know it can be very frustrating when people are talking or moving about in the service while I am up teaching. So I can imagine how Paul felt, he was no different. So I believe Paul got frustrated and out of frustration he digressed from his teaching and said, *"let your women keep silence in the churches: for it is not permitted unto them to speak;"*. Why? Because you women *(wives)* are being very disruptive. Paul went on to say to them all, *"it is not permitted for them* [wives] *to speak"*.

Now I know what you're thinking, how do you know Paul digressed from his teaching? I'm glad you asked the question. All you have to do is look at what he was talking about in verse 32 and 33 *"And the spirits of the prophets are subject to the prophets. 33 For God is not the author of confusion, but of peace, as in all churches of the saints"*. Then Paul goes totally off-topic and starts talking about these rowdy women *(no offense intended)*, *"let your women keep silence in the churches..., ...for it is a shame for women to speak in the church"*. This statement has nothing to do with what he was talking about earlier; *"the spirit of the prophets"*. When he had finished dealing with this distraction, he got right back on topic in verses *36 "What? came the word of God out from you? or came it unto you only? 37 If any man think himself to be a prophet…".*. See he goes right back to the original topic that he had been speaking on. Paul was no different than preachers today, sometimes having to digress in our teaching to deal with a distraction such as a crying baby in the service, and then continue back on topic in our teaching. I believe Paul did just that, he stopped teaching, took care of the distraction at hand and then started back right where he left off.

He wasn't talking to all women when he said *"let your women keep silence in the churches",* he was only talking to the wives because of their Jewish religious traditions. Again, if Paul was talking about all women then I guess the single women are supposed to stay ignorant and dumb. Single women will never learn anything, because they don't have a husband at home to ask. This means they can't learn anything until they get married then they can ask their own husbands at home. Give me a break!!! That is about the second dumbest thing I've ever heard.

To think that Paul was talking about all *"women keep silence in the churches"* is dumb, especially when Paul himself had women helping him in the ministry. Look at these verses in the 18th chapter of Acts; verse 18 says, *"And Paul after this tarried there* [at Achaia] *yet a good while, and then took his leave of the brethren, and sailed thence into Syria, and with him Priscilla and Aquila; having shorn his head in Cenchrea: for he had a vow. 19 And he came to Ephesus, and left them* [Priscilla and Aquila] *there… .* Now look at verse 26 *And he* [Apollos] *began to speak boldly in the synagogue: whom when Aquila and Priscilla had heard, they took him unto them, and expounded* [explain] *unto him the way of God more perfectly".*

"Apollos knowing only the baptism of John" (Acts 18:25), or what John The Baptist preached, but was not

knowledgeable about the baptism of Christ. Apollos did know about what Jesus had done, but he did not know about the death, burial and resurrection. However, because of Paul's teaching Priscilla and Aquila did know and they took Apollos and instructed and explained to him salvation, a more perfect way, the baptism of Christ. If Paul meant for all women to keep silent in the church, why is he allowing this man and his wife to assist him in the ministry, by instructing or teaching others?

Let's read on. In Romans 16:1-5 it says, *"I commend unto you Phebe our sister, which is a servant of the church which is at Cenchrea: 2 That ye receive her in the Lord, as becometh saints, and that ye assist her in whatsoever business she hath need of you: for she hath been a succourer of many, and of myself also. 3 Greet Priscilla and Aquila my helpers in Christ Jesus: 4 Who have for my life laid down their own necks: unto whom not only I give thanks, but also all the churches of the Gentiles. Likewise greet the church* [the body of Christ] *that is in their house".* If you read on in this 16th chapter you will see that there were other women that assisted Paul in the ministry also.

Look at what Paul goes on to say in 1 Corinthians 16:19-20 *"The churches of Asia salute you. Aquila and Priscilla salute you much in the Lord, with the church that is in their house. 20 All the brethren greet you. Greet ye one another with an holy kiss".* Paul spoke highly of this woman *Priscilla* and her husband. They had to be doing a good job for Paul to say in verse 20 *"all the brethren greet you".* He went on to speak highly about two other women's sincere faith, Timothy's *"grandmother Lois and his mother Eunice"* (2 Timothy 1:5). Paul didn't have a problem with women teaching and preaching in the church, but there are some preachers today that still have a problem with this, and that's why they make such a big deal about 1 Corinthians 14:34.

You can see from these passages of scripture Paul was

not talking about all *"women keep silence in the churches"*, he was only talking about wives at that time, because of their religious traditions. *"Women keep silence in the churches"*, why should they, especially when some are doing a better job than some men?

CHAPTER 6

The Days of Our Years- Man's life is more than 70 or 80
years:

*Psalms 90:10 The days of our years are threescore years and ten; and
if by reason of strength they be fourscore years…*

Preachers have taken this scripture and taught it for
years that we will only live seventy to eighty years. I have
even taught it myself. But I submit unto you that this is
not biblically true. You must change your way of thinking.
Because if your thinking is wrong, it's going to affect how
you believe, and if your believing is wrong it is going to
affect your confession *(what you say)*. If you think that you
will only live seventy to eighty years, then that's what
you're going to believe and that's what you're going to
confess, and that's what you're going to have. God said, *for
as he* (a man) *thinketh in his heart, so is he (Proverbs 23:7).*
Whatever is in your heart *(your spirit)* it's going to come out
of your mouth. Jesus said, *for out of the abundance of the heart
the mouth speaketh (Matthew 12:34).* So, you have to control
what goes into your heart, and you do that by controlling
what you hear, because *faith cometh by hearing… (Romans*

27

10:17). Faith for anything comes by hearing, and if you continue to hear the wrong things you are going to have faith for those things.

You have a covenant with God that promises you long life, and that long life is more than seventy or eighty years. When I or others speak of covenant, most Christians have no idea what we are talking about. The sad thing is that Christians, church people, not the worldly people, but the Christians, don't even know that they have *a better covenant, which was established upon better promises (Hebrews 8:6).* We have a better covenant, better than the one Abraham had. *Genesis 24:34-35 says, And he said, I am Abraham's servant. 35 And the Lord hath blessed my master greatly; and he is become great: and he hath given him flocks, and herds, and silver, and gold, and menservants, and maidservants, and camels, and asses.* Abraham sent his servant out to find a wife for his son Isaac. When he came to the well and was talking to Rebecca there, he started telling her how God had blessed his master greatly. Abraham had a pretty good covenant, and God blessed him with everything he needed physically. Not only did God bless him materially but God also blessed him with long life. *Abraham lived one hundred and seventy five years before he died.*

7 And these are the days of the years of Abraham's life which he lived, an hundred threescore and fifteen [175] years. 8 Then Abraham gave up the ghost, and died in a good old age, an old man, and full of years (Genesis 25:7-8). Look at all that Abraham had in his covenant including long life, and we *(Christians),* have a better covenant established upon better promises and don't even know it. Hosea 4:6 says, *my people are destroyed for lack of knowledge... .* You can't operate in something that you have no knowledge in. If you don't know what God has promised you, how can you operate in it? You can't!!! The Bible speaks of over eight thousand promises that God has given us. When it comes to God, a promise is a covenant, an agreement, and He does not take it back. If God has given us over eight thousand promises, don't you think it's important that you and I know and understand these promises so that we can take full advantage of them? Do you remember the definition that I gave you of the word "covenant"? *An agreement, undertaking, commitment, guarantee, warrant, pledge, promise, bond.* This is how God views a covenant, and He doesn't change it.

Let me digress for a few minutes and talk about covenant, maybe it would help you to better understand what you have. As I stated earlier in chapter one; some have thought that when Jesus hung on the cross and said, *...it is finished...* *(John 19:30)* he was talking about salvation and man's redemption, but He wasn't. He was talking about the old covenant dispensation *(the Old Testament)*, the law, it was finished. Everything that God had promised was fulfilled when Jesus hung on the cross. That's why He said *it is finished and he bowed his head, and gave up the ghost.* He fulfilled it, the Old Covenant, it was over. So, from the point of Jesus giving up the ghost, until He rose from the dead three days later alive, the people had no covenant, it was fulfilled. Consider this, which you have probably never given consideration to: The people had no promise, no agreement, no covenant from God for three days and three nights. They had no guarantee from God for anything until Jesus rose from the dead alive and God established a new covenant, a better covenant established upon better promises.

There are four important reasons why we should understand Covenant:

> 1. We learn that God deals with man through covenants. The Bible is a book of Covenants:
>   **a.** Covenant between "God and man".
>   **b.** Covenant between "man and man".

    c. Covenant between "a leader and his people".

    d. Covenant between "nations".

2. Covenant is an agreement, it is a promise made by God, and we can rely on His word, promising us eternal life through His Son Jesus Christ.

3. It helps us to see the bible as a covenant document. The Old and New Testaments are Old and New Covenants, it's a legal term.

4. When we understand Covenant, we can better understand our responsibilities to God as well as His responsibilities to us.

The Bible is broken down into two types of Covenants, *Conditional* and *Unconditional.* God has made both types of covenant with his people. Covenant is how God chose to redeem us, communicate with us and guarantee us eternal life through Jesus Christ.

Conditional Covenant – *is an agreement between two parties where conditions are placed upon each party.* It refers to an agreement that is binding on both parties for its fulfillment. If either party fails to meet their responsibilities, the covenant is broken and therefore neither party then has to fulfill the expectations of the covenant.

Example:
Genesis 2:16-17 *God said, …Of every tree of the garden thou mayest freely eat… But of the tree of the knowledge of good and evil, thou shalt not eat…,* man's part of the covenant is to obey and not eat in order to obtain the benefits. Genesis 12:1-3 *Now the Lord said, …get thee out of thy country…,* man's part of the covenant is to obey and get out of his country in order to obtain the benefits and in return God's part is; *and I will*

bless thee...

Malachi 3:10-12 *Bring ye all the tithes into the storehouse...* man's part of the covenant is to obey and bring all the tithes into the storehouse in order to obtain the benefits, and in return God's part is; *and I will rebuke the devourer for your sakes.... And all nations shall call you blessed...*

Conditional covenants require each party to do something in order for them to obtain the benefits of it.

Unconditional Covenant – *is an agreement between two parties where only one of the two parties has to do something, and nothing is required of the other party.*

Example:
Genesis 1:26-31 *And God said, Let us make man in our image, after our likeness: and let them have dominion over the fish of the sea... So God created man in his own image... and blessed them...* Man didn't have to do anything in order to obtain the benefits.
2 Peter 1:2-4 *...According as his divine power hath given unto us all things that pertain unto life and godliness... Whereby are given unto us exceeding great and precious promises....* Christians have to do nothing else to obtain the benefits.

God has done everything He's going to do, He is at rest *(ceased from work).* Hebrews 4:4 says, *...And God did rest the seventh day from all his works.* God is at rest and He has already done His part of the covenant. He is now waiting on you to do your part so you can obtain the benefits of it. God wants you to enter into His rest. Hebrews 4:10 says, *For he that is entered into his rest, he also hath ceased from his own works, as God did from his.* Psalms 37:7 says, *Rest in the LORD, and wait patiently for him....* 'Rest' means to cease from work or labor. When you live according to God's covenant, your life will be restful and not stressful, because stress is work.

Now that you understand covenant, let's go back to "The Days of Our Years".

Consider this: 2 Corinthians 1:20 says, *For all the promises of God in him are yea* [yes], *and in him Amen, unto the glory of God by us.* Amen means *"so be it".* If God has promised it, it is so. Not maybe so, not hope so, it is so because He said it was. God doesn't change His mind like you do. One day you are up, the next day you are down, one day you are smiling with me, the next day you are talking about me. God is consistent *(holding firmly)* to His promises. Malachi 3:6 says, *For I am the LORD, I change not...,* and Hebrews 13:8 says, *Jesus Christ the same yesterday, and to day, and for ever.* So, that tells me that God has not changed his mind about the number of man's days. He has promised us *one hundred and twenty* years of life, so we must start believing and confessing what He has promised us in order to live the full number of our days. *And the LORD said, My spirit shall not always strive with man, for that he also is flesh: yet his days shall be an hundred and twenty years (Genesis 6:3).* That's a promise!!! Not just seventy or eighty years, but if that's all you want to live, God will let you do that because you have a choice to believe Him or not to believe Him.

Exodus 23:25-26 says, *And ye shall serve the LORD your God, and he shall bless thy bread, and thy water; and I will take sickness away from the midst of thee. 26 There shall nothing cast their young, nor be barren, in thy land: the number of thy days I will fulfill.* This is a promise from God, but in order to achieve it you must believe and confess it daily by faith. *Death and life are in the power of the tongue (Proverbs 18:21).* God doesn't change like man changes. Romans 11:29 says, *For the gifts and calling of God are without repentance* [to change]. Psalms 91:14-16 says, *Because he hath set his love upon me, therefore will I deliver him: I will set him on high, because he hath known my name.*

15 He shall call upon me, and I will answer him: I will be with him in trouble; I will deliver him, and honour him. 16 With long life will I satisfy him, and shew him my salvation. This is based on you knowing your covenant rights and standing on them in faith. Again, you can't operate in something you have no knowledge in. Hosea 4:6 says, *My people are destroyed for lack of knowledge... .* You have to know God's ways in order to stand on his promises. So, I ask you the question; what is God capable of doing? The children of Israel knew God's acts, but Moses knew God's ways. Do you know God's ways? Do you know what God will do or won't do?

We have example after example throughout the Bible of people that have obeyed God's word, and lived one *hundred twenty years* or more:

The Death of Sarah:

Sarah lived one hundred and twenty-seven years before she died.
Genesis *23:1 And Sarah was an hundred and seven and twenty years old these were the years of the life of Sarah.*

The Death of Abraham:

Abraham lived one hundred and seventy-five years before he died.
Genesis 25:7-8 *And these are the days of the years of Abraham's life which he lived, an hundred threescore and fifteen years. 8 Then Abraham gave up the ghost, and died in a good old age, an old man, and full of years; and was gathered to his people.*

The Death of Isaac:

Isaac *lived one hundred and eighty years before he died.*
Genesis 35:28-29 *And the days of Isaac were an hundred and fourscore years. 29 And Isaac gave up the ghost, and died, and was*

gathered unto his people, being old and full of days…

The Death of Jacob:

Jacob *lived one hundred and forty-seven years before he died.*
Gen. 47:28 *so the whole age of Jacob was an hundred forty and seven years.*

The Death of Aaron:

Aaron *lived one hundred and twenty-three years before he died.*
Numbers 33:39 *And Aaron was an hundred and twenty and three years old when he died…*

The Death of Moses:

Moses *lived one hundred and twenty years before he died.*
Deuteronomy 34:7 *And Moses was an hundred and twenty years old when he died: his eye was not dim, nor his natural force abated.*

Yes, I know, there are many others in the Bible that lived beyond one hundred and twenty years. Yet there are many others in the Bible that did not live to see one hundred and twenty years. Why is that? I don't know!!! Maybe they missed something, because God can't miss. But that doesn't mean that God changed his mind about the number of man's days.

Remember what I am talking about in this book, "breaking traditions". I want to deal with something that I have heard people say that is very misleading, and it will affect how you believe. Listening to this kind of talk will make your faith weak, because faith cometh by what you hear.

People will say that when your time is up, no matter your age, God is going to take you, because He doesn't make mistakes. When your number is up, it's up, no matter what. Or they will say God won't put any more on you than you can bear. None of this is biblically true!!! I haven't found any of that in the Bible, or anywhere in the covenant that God has given us. Again, you have to know your covenant rights in order to take full advantage of what is yours. God never took anyone dead, He always took them alive. There are three people in the Bible that did not see death, God took them but He took them alive. Enoch always walked in faith, and it was well pleasing to God. So, God gave the man what he wanted. Enoch didn't see death, ...*God took him (Genesis 5:24)*. He didn't die physically, God took him. Likewise Elijah, God took Elijah ...*there appeared a chariot of fire, and horses of fire...*, ...*and Elijah went up by a whirlwind into heaven (2 Kings 2:11)*, God took him. And then there was Jesus Christ. He preached his last message to His disciples on the Mount of Olives, ...*while they beheld, he was taken up; and a cloud received him out of their sight (Acts 1:9)*, God took Him. Notice how God took them, he took them alive, not dead, and He hasn't taken any one else since..

The Bible refers to us, the Christians, as going to sleep, not dying. Stop saying that God took your loved ones, He did not. You might say, what happened to my loved ones if God didn't take them? Why did they die an early death? No one knows how a person lives their life outside of the public eye, behind closed doors. You don't know what they have been believing and confessing. Maybe they were ready to go, you don't really know. What have you been believing and confessing? Are you confessing what God has promised, long life, one hundred and twenty years? If not, maybe and I say just maybe that's why people are not living the full life that God has promised. Make no mistake about it, sin will shorten your life, and anything opposite of what God has said or has commanded us to do is sin even if you are doing it out of tradition.

Remember I brought out in the introduction; Mark 7:9, 13 it says, *…you reject the commandment of God, that ye may keep your own tradition. 13 Making the word of God of none effect through your tradition… .* Jesus was letting the people know that not all traditions are good, especially when it causes you not to keep the commandments of God. If you are not keeping the commandments of God, that means you are sinning, and there is no in-between. Numbers 32:22 says, *But if ye will not do so, behold, ye have sinned against the Lord: and be sure your sin will find you out.* Sure 1 John 1:9 says, *If we confess our sins, he is faithful and just to forgive us our sins, and to cleanse us from all unrighteousness.* Yes, He will forgive you if you ask, thank God for that. But remember Galatians 6:7-8 says, *…whatsoever a man soweth, that shall he also reap. 8 For he that soweth to his flesh shall of the flesh reap corruption; but he that soweth to the Spirit shall of the Spirit reap life everlasting.* Don't let your traditions make the word of God of none effect *[vain; fruitless]* in your life. If you desire to live beyond seventy or eighty years, then according to your faith, live on!!!

CHAPTER 7

Christmas – Who was at the Manger in the Stable?

Many people have followed certain Christmas traditions simply because it's always been done that way or because the story of the birth of Christ has always been told that way, but they have never taken the time to see whether or not these things are true. There are certain Christmas traditions that I want to deal with that are not biblical truths. I want to show you what the bible says and help you break these traditions. Every year around Christmas time as I drive around I see the nativity scenes that people have set up in their yards and even out in front of churches that are not true. They will have the nativity scene with Joseph, Mary and the baby Jesus laying in the manger in the stable. There will also be some animals around the stable, and three wise men or three kings. This is not biblically true, the wise men never saw the infant baby Jesus lying in the manger at the stable. Let me prove it with the scripture;

Matthew 2:1-16 says, 1 Now when Jesus was born in Bethlehem of Judaea in the days of Herod the king, behold, there came wise men from the east to Jerusalem, 2 Saying, Where is he that is born King of the Jews? for we have seen his star in the east, and are come to worship him. 3 When Herod the king had heard these things, he was troubled, and all Jerusalem with him. 4 And when he had gathered all the chief priests and scribes of the people together, he demanded of them where Christ should be born. 5 And they said unto him, In Bethlehem of Judaea: for thus it is written by the prophet, 6 And thou Bethlehem, in the land of Juda, art not the least among the princes of Juda: for out of thee shall come a Governor, that shall rule my people Israel. 7 Then Herod, when he had privily called the wise men, enquired of them diligently what time the star appeared. 8 And he sent them to Bethlehem, and said, Go and search diligently for the young child; and when ye have found him, bring me word again, that I may come and worship him also. 9 When they had heard the king, they departed; and, lo, the star, which they saw in the east, went before them, till it came and stood over where the young child was. 10 When they saw the star, they rejoiced with exceeding great joy. 11 And when they were come into the house, they saw the young child with Mary his mother, and fell down, and worshipped him: and when they had opened their treasures, they presented unto him gifts; gold, and frankincense, and myrrh. 12 And being warned of God in a dream that they should not return to Herod, they departed into their own country another way. 13 And when they were departed, behold, the angel of the Lord appeareth to Joseph in a dream, saying, Arise, and take the young child and his mother, and flee into Egypt, and be thou there until I bring thee word: for Herod will seek the young child to destroy him. 14 When he arose, he took the young child and his mother by night, and departed into Egypt: 15 And was there until the death of Herod: that it might be fulfilled which was spoken of the Lord by the prophet, saying, Out of Egypt have I called my son. 16 Then Herod, when he saw that he was mocked of the wise men, was exceeding wroth, and sent forth, and slew all the children that were in Bethlehem, and in all the coasts thereof, from two years old and under, according to the time which he had diligently enquired of the wise men.

Let's go back and look at what this is saying. Notice it

says in verse one *there came wise men from the east to Jerusalem.* It doesn't say three wise men, it just says wise men, now it could have been three, or it could have been two, but it could have been fifty or more, it just says wise men, so we know it was at least two. I believe that it was very unlikely that there were only two or three men traveling alone. In those days when people traveled they traveled in *a company of people* called a caravan. They traveled together for safety reasons. There were thieves, robbers and killers out on the road ready to rob and kill people at any given time, so traveling in numbers was the safest thing to do. So, the wise men would have never been traveling with just two or three men, that would have been very unsafe. They were called wise men for a reason. I believe people say three wise men because of the three gifts that were given in verse eleven, but that doesn't mean that it was three men. One could have given all three gifts or two could have given the three gifts, and the other one could have come empty-handed like some church folks do when they come to church. You just don't know, so don't get locked in on three. Next, notice that they traveled from the east a long way off. Now skip to verse eleven and notice what it says, *and when they were come into the house.* They who? The wise men, notice they didn't come in to the stable, they came into the house. *When they came into the house they saw the young child with Mary his mother..., ...when they had opened their treasures, they presented unto him gifts; gold, and frankincense, and myrrh.* Like I mentioned earlier, this is where people get the three wise men from, because they gave three gifts. The wise men never saw the infant baby Jesus lying in a manger at the stable, because by the time they had arrived to Jerusalem at least two years had passed. We know that because of what Herod the king said and did in verse sixteen; it says, *Herod, when he saw that he was mocked of the wise men,* mocked means tricked or made a fool of by them. God warned them in a dream not to go back to Herod, but go back to their own country a different way *(verse 12).*

Herod was so mad he *sent forth, and slew all the children that were in Bethlehem, and in all the coasts thereof, from two years old and under, according to the time which he had diligently enquired of the wise men.* Go back to verse seven, he *enquired of them diligently what time the star appeared... .* Herod was no dummy, he knew from the time that the star had appeared until the time that it took the wise men to travel from the east to Jerusalem, at least two years had passed. Travel in those days was very slow, they didn't have trains, planes or automobiles. A day's journey was considered 20 miles, so it took them a very long time to get there. That's why according to verse sixteen Herod slew all the children *from two years old and under.* You don't kill a two-year-old young child trying to kill an infant baby. This is not a play on words!!! Notice in these passages of scripture the term *"young child"* was mentioned six times. Matthew was making a distinction between a young child and an infant baby, so you would know the difference.

Never put out a nativity scene with the three wise men at the manger in the stable, because according to the scriptures they were never there. They never saw the infant baby Jesus lying in a manger in the stable. Don't you think Joseph had enough sense to get his wife and baby out of the stable, and move them into a house after she gave birth? That's why it says in the scripture, and when they (the *wise men) were come into the house,* that was some two years later after the birth of Christ. Now there were people there at the manger in the stable, but it was the shepherds, not wise men. *And it came to pass, as the angels were gone away from them into heaven, the shepherds said one to another, Let us now go even unto Bethlehem, and see this thing which is come to pass, which the Lord hath made known unto us. And they came with haste, and found Mary, and Joseph, and the babe lying in a manger (Luke 2:15-16).*

These have been things to make you go hmmm!!! It's a

40

different view, and it's for your consideration so you can break traditions. Remember change, it begins with you.

ABOUT THE AUTHOR

Dr. Jake Williams Jr. was born and raised in Seale, AL. He graduated high school in 1975, and joined the military in 1976 where he served 22 years in the U.S. Army before retiring in 1998. Dr. Williams received his called into the ministry in 1989 at Jesus World Outreach Center in Heilbron, Germany (which is now located in Heidelberg, Germany). In September 1997, he founded the Fayetteville, NC branch of Jesus World Outreach Center, Inc. (JWOC) under the Spirit-filled leadership of Apostles Elisha and Phyllis Lawson. He earned an Associate degree in General Education from Fayetteville Technical Community College, a Bachelor in Bible, a Master in Theology and a Doctorate in Christian Education from Great Commission Bible College and Seminary. He is an accomplished commercial pilot, founder and overseer of the JWOC Angel Flight Program where he gives back to the community by flying disabled veterans to various locations free of charge. He is also the founder and overseer of a men's ministry called Men of Integrity where he teaches men to walk in their integrity enabling them to take back their rightful places as men, husbands, and fathers in the home. He has a sincere heart for helping people and making them disciples of Jesus Christ. Dr. Williams is a radical mighty man of God who travels with his wife nationally and internationally teaching the uncompromising Word of God.